Anders Ericsson & Robert Pools

PEAK

Secrets from the
New Science of Expertise

Summary by Ant Hive Media

Copyright © 2016 by Ant Hive Media

Please Note

This is a Summary & Analysis of the original book, available here: http://amzn.to/2bX8eU8. Or, visit http://amzn.to/1WpoTBi for easy listening.

You can get two Audio Books of your choice FREE with Audible now. Simply start your digital membership here: http://amzn.to/1WpoTBi and choose the books you want.

Copyright © 2016 by Ant Hive Media

All rights reserved worldwide. No part of this publication may be reproduced or transmitted in any form without the prior written consent of the publisher

Disclaimer:

The fact that an individual or organization is referred to in this document as a citation or source of information does not imply that the author or publisher endorses the information that the individual or organization provided. This concise summary is not intended to be used without reference to the original book

Table of Contents

A GIFT FOR YOU

SUMMARY 1

CORE CONCEPTS 3

ANALYSIS OF CORE CONCEPTS 4

CORE CONCEPT 1:
GENIUSES ARE NOT BORN; THEY ARE MADE. 4

CORE CONCEPT 2:
THE MATURE BRAIN CONTINUES TO BE ADAPTABLE. THEREFORE, IT IS WRONG TO SAY THAT ONLY YOUNG PEOPLE CAN BE TRAINED. 6

CORE CONCEPT 3:
DELIBERATE PRACTICE IS A SURE WAY TO BECOMING AN EXPERT OR TOP PERFORMER. 7

CORE CONCEPT 4:
DELIBERATE PRACTICE IS ABOUT RECOGNIZING MENTAL PATTERNS AS MUCH AS REPETITIVE DRILLS. 9

CORE CONCEPT 5:
DELIBERATE PRACTICE IS LEARNING BY DOING, NOT SIMPLY BY KNOWING. 11

CORE CONCEPT 6:
PURPOSEFUL TRAINING IS ABOUT PUSHING STUDENTS BEYOND THEIR LIMITS. 13

CORE CONCEPT 7:
AN EXPERT INSTRUCTOR IS ESSENTIAL TO PURPOSEFUL TRAINING. 14

CORE CONCEPT 8:
THE LENGTH OF PRACTICE DOES NOT GUARANTEE EXPERTISE; IT IS DELIBERATE PRACTICE OVER TIME THAT COUNTS. 15

CORE CONCEPT 9:
DELIBERATE PRACTICE IS MORE IMPORTANT NOW THAN EVER BECAUSE THE ECONOMY HAS CHANGED SUCH THAT WORKERS MUST CONSTANTLY LEARN AND EXCEL IN NEW SKILLSETS TO STAY RELEVANT. 17

AUTHOR'S STYLE 18

AUTHOR'S PERSPECTIVE 19

CONNECT WITH ANT HIVE MEDIA! 20

THANK YOU FOR READING! 20

WANT MORE? 20

CUSTOMERS WHO BOUGHT THIS SUMMARY ALSO BOUGHT 21

A Gift for You

As a way of saying thank you we want to offer you a pack of (5) e-book summaries **FREE!**

Available Here:
www.anthivemedia.com/freesummaries

SUMMARY

Can expertise be achieved or is it only for the naturally gifted? Peak: Secrets from the New Science of Expertise gives a factual look into the phenomenon of top performers.

Practice is at the heart of every excellent performance. In fact, Ericsson believes genius is not born; it is made through purposeful practice. For instance, Mozart, long considered a child prodigy with signs of exceptional musicality, had to undergo deliberate music training, a decision of his father who was also a musician. At seven years old, Mozart was the toast of the European elite, but few knew that the innate musical skills of Mozart was highly re-enforced by a very purposeful and rigorous music education.

The decision to develop a person's set of skills in a particular field of discipline to the point of expertise should not be based on signs of exceptional skills early on into a person's life. This kind of mindset is wrong. If a program of purposeful training results in excellent competencies, the initial achievement or non-achievement of a child or a neophyte in a particular discipline should not be the basis for making the decision on whether or not training matters for them.

Deliberate practice is not synonymous with incredibly long and grueling hours of practice, much less unstructured training. It is not about systematic thinking each time they use their craft or skill to perform a difficult task. Rather it zeroes in on a structured training regimen which includes a rigid mental training that develops precise recognition, recall, and application of mental patterns. In addition, an expert teacher is at the heart of a successful education of a student. The mentor can share and transfer vast knowledge and skills to the trainee who, by the way, need not always be a child.

Yet, people have still to appreciate the power of purposeful training. Nonetheless, once this technique is popularized it can only mean more experts around us. For instance, expect a significant and marked decrease in errors in the field of medicine should doctors undergo on-going deliberate practice. In addition, should formal education consider adopting the techniques of deliberate practice in their curriculum, they can only look forward to more children not only learning skills faster, but developing them to the level of expertise.

Important People

K. Anders Ericsson is a psychologist and scholar and psychology professor. He is internationally recognized as a researcher in the psychological nature of expertise and human performance. Peak extensively discusses his concept of purposeful training as an effective way to develop top performers.

Robert Pool co-wrote Peak. He is an author and screenwriter specializing in science and technology. He worked as staff for the magazines Science, and Nature.

CORE CONCEPTS

1. Geniuses are not born; they are made.
2. The mature brain continues to be adaptable. Therefore, it is wrong to say that only young people can be trained.
3. Purposeful training is a sure way to becoming a top performer.
4. Purposeful drills are about recognizing mental patterns as much as learning to use them.
5. Purposeful practice is learning by doing, not simply knowing.
6. Purposeful training is about pushing students beyond their limits.
7. An expert instructor is essential to purposeful training.
8. The length of practice does not guarantee expertise; it is deliberate practice over time that counts.
9. Deliberate practice is highly relevant in our modern age which constantly evolves and requires persons with up dated skill sets.

ANALYSIS OF CORE CONCEPTS

Core Concept 1:

Geniuses are not born; they are made.

The notion that geniuses are born is questionable. Additionally, it is unfair to a child who may not be perceived as skilled at birth. Teachers and experts who expect a naturally talented child to excel early on without practice are usually biased against training an average child to be a top performer. However, the decision to be an expert should be a choice and not determined by birth.

It seems gifted persons have everything going for them. A University College of London study revealed a bias for people who were believed to have innate talents compared to those who were successful through hard work. The researchers gave investors a fictional profile of business men. Some were described as naturally gifted while others were portrayed as hard workers based on their IQ levels and leadership skills. The research showed that although the hard workers were exemplary achievers as well, yet a large majority of the investors opted for the businessmen who were innately talented.

Nonetheless, despite this preference for gifted persons, the fact is that even slow beginners overtake or surpass the achievements of people who are naturally gifted. Apparently the naturally talented often fail to diligently work on polishing their skills as compared to their supposedly weaker counterparts.

It is even possible that over time the gifted may have to struggle to succeed. The stumbling block is their fear of failure and the pressure to achieve given their exceptionally high IQs. On the contrary, the average person simply concentrates on studying or training without the pressure of delivering exceptional results. While too much premium is given on IQ levels in determining a person's skills, IQ scores do not truly measure the intelligence of a person.

Core Concept 2:

The mature brain continues to be adaptable. Therefore, it is wrong to say that only young people can be trained.

The adage that you cannot teach old dog new tricks is not true, particularly when referring to the adult brain. Previously it was believed that the adaptability of the brain is a characteristic of only young people which is behind the belief that they quickly learn or acquire skills. Yet, except for disciplines that require exceptional physical strength, older people are just as capable of building and acquiring new competencies that involve mental skills, sometimes even more than the very young. The brain of an adult continually re-generates under the best or worst circumstances. For instance, a 2013 study established the effect of radioactive elements on the human brain using as reference point a benchmark level of radioactivity in brain cells after a nuclear disaster. The study revealed that neurons regenerated in the adult brain at a rate of 700 cells a day debunking the belief that, at a given point, mature brains stop growing and atrophy with the passing of time.

Core Concept 3:

Deliberate practice is a sure way to becoming an expert or top performer.

Repetition of a desired skill for countless hours daily is not enough to become an expert. For instance, a piano student who limits his practice to only one musical score will never move on to more complicated sonatas. Purposeful practice is a systematic regimen in cultivating a target skill. In all areas of expertise, it adopts a proven method that students who are training to be top performers can adopt and eventually learn from.

Take Michael Phelps, the swimming legend who established a world record of 23 gold medals in the recently concluded Rio Olympics. It is already a bonus that he has a body build that gives him a natural advantage as a swimmer. His impressive height— 1.93meters, gives him a 6-foot-7 spread between the tips of his arms. But this would be of not much help without the rigorous training Phelps imposes on himself. He literally dives into methodical training for every competition, but training is not about spending countless hours in the pool. While he recommends this for endurance, he couples it with "painful" drills each day which he does to bring his skills to perfection. It is not just physical endurance—at times beyond any limits, but mental training is just as important. In 2008 Beijing Olympics, there was one event when Phelps's goggles filled up with water. But Phelps maintained his presence of mind and mentally noted the number of strokes he still had to make before he makes his turns—and he won despite the problem.

Core Concept 4:

Deliberate practice is about recognizing mental patterns as much as repetitive drills.

Apparently, recognizing patterns is the key to making fast and effective mental and physical performances. These patterns are the mental short cuts that effectively reduce the problems of short-term memory or the conventional step-by-step mental processes. To illustrate, a doctor who after years of honing the skill of noting symptoms and associating them with particular diseases, arrives at a correct diagnosis—without having to go through the standard procedure of diagnostics. The same principle applies to a skier. He can look at a terrain for the first time, but by mentally recalling scenarios he has acquired from long hours of practice, he produces a plan to quickly and safely navigate the route.

Some industries rely on expertise that requires extremely sharp mental skills. For instance, the ability to identify the gender of a chick practically right after it is hatched is not only rare but enormously valued. Egg farms need people with the unique skill to tell a female from a male chick as only female chicks are needed on the farm. The problem is a chick has its genitals hidden inside its body which makes gender recognition difficult. Chick sexers are highly trained to do just that. Often, they have to go through three-year training before they are given the task to desegregate thousands of female from male chicks each day. To the non-trained eye the difference is almost impossible to note, but years of rigorous training has taught chick sexers to automatically know, in seconds, which is male or female— all from training on recognizing mental representations.

Core Concept 5:

Deliberate practice is learning by doing, not simply by knowing.

Formal education is associated with classroom-based learning. This is the system from early education to university education including continuing education that medical professionals undergo. Doctors, for instance, attend seminars and conferences to keep abreast of the latest developments in the field of medical science. But nothing beats hands-on training. Hours spent on purposeful practice are without doubt more effective in developing competent medical practitioners rather than having them sit down and listen to hours of tedious lectures.

The myth about learning through traditional teaching methods, where the teacher is the center of classroom activities and the students are passive learners, has long been discarded. A 2011 study on effective teaching methods revealed that students who learned through active classroom teaching-learning strategies received higher evaluation scores compared with those who learned from traditional methods, such as lectures and other teacher-centered activities

Active learning, which is task-oriented, must be adopted by keeping the learning continuum of dependence to independence in mind. For instance, a medical student learns to perform surgery through the expert guidance of his medical professor. The process begins from close supervision to gradual withdrawal and, finally, total independence of the medical student in performing an operation. Effective learning, however, cannot be exclusively attributed to hands-on training. For instance, chess can be learned by reading the various moves of chess masters; or by observing the experts and noting patterns of the game, a chess enthusiast can graduate into a chess expert.

Core Concept 6:

Purposeful training is about pushing students beyond their limits.

The body always seeks physiological equilibrium. This orientation toward balance is behind the adaptability of people to new mental and physical skills. But this can also work against the learning progress of students since it leads to plateaus of skills which students might find comfort in settling in. The challenge, therefore, is not to achieve the comfortable zone of a skill but to push harder to yet higher levels via new approaches to their craft. Again, training hard is not enough; there should be a variety of training techniques.

CrossFit perfectly illustrates this idea as a CrossFit regimen is never duplicated. The point is to give them different workouts so that they don't get used to just one task. In fact, Greg Glassman, the founder of CrossFit describes his exercise regimen as a sequence of different functional movements. At CrossFit the mantra is: Routine is the enemy. The final goal is not to condition the body from adopting predictable movements or exercises, but to anticipate instead new functions and tasks thereby becoming an expert over time on a skill set.

Core Concept 7:

An expert instructor is essential to purposeful training.

An expert trainer is a must to purposeful training, although for unorthodox or novel skills, it may not always happen that a student finds a masterful mentor. Certainly, nothing beats skills learned from an expert in the field who can transfer age-old honed skills effectively through deliberate practice. It is best to look for the wisdom of the past for without it progress can be illusive. Nonetheless, individuals who cannot find an expert trainer can turn the situation into a challenge to be top performers through self-training.

Coach Béla Károlyi is associated with Olympic success in the field of gymnastics. One of his paramount achievements is Nadia Comaneci who got a perfect score in the 1976 Montreal Olympics. Karolyi together with his wife has developed their training program to perfection—adopted from the government-prescribed regimen in Romania. While their critics don't quite agree with the harsh even brutal nature of Karolyi's practice methods, but top performers like Kerri Strug believe that though training with him is not a walk in the park it does produce excellent results.

Core Concept 8:

The length of practice does not guarantee expertise; it is deliberate practice over time that counts.

Thousands of hours of training do not make a top performer. This is contrary to what Malcolm Gladwell proposed in his book, Outliers. Practicing for thousands of hours —10,000 hours to be exact, according to Gladwell—is not the road to becoming an expert; nor is thousands of hours of practice necessary. In fact, there is no prescribed number of hours of training that would guarantee expertise in a particular discipline. It could mean shorter or longer hours of training. In some cases, when people achieve a certain level of expertise they plateau and stay comfortable in that level. What is essential is focused practice, otherwise one may never achieve expert status.

Deliberate practice significantly differs from conventional training. Take the case of two runners. They have the same number of hours of daily training. However, Runner A limits himself to a standard outdoor routine on the same route each day. Runner B divides his daily training between running different routes and spending the rest of his practice on gym work. Runner A may not think highly of his co-trainee for not maximizing his running routine. Runner B, however, is on a deliberate program. He combines experience from his varied routes and incorporates them to his other training regimens. It is not surprising that Runner B will win a contest hands down anytime between him and Runner A—even if Runner A trains for 10,000 hours.

Core Concept 9:

Deliberate practice is more important now than ever because the economy has changed such that workers must constantly learn and excel in new skillsets to stay relevant.

Our schools and workplaces can learn from the methods used in deliberate practice. Purposeful training can be a highly effective strategy in transferring knowledge and skills better and faster to school children. In the workplace, it will make people relevant despite the advances in technology.

Switching jobs is now the new normal. In the recent past, job hopping was a stigma and a person in the job market who has multiple jobs behind him had to live down dependability and loyalty issues. Surprisingly, companies nowadays have a more positive attitude toward job switching. Patty McCord, previously the talent officer at Netflix, believes job switching reflects a person's adaptability and a faster learning curve. Those who stay on the job for long periods are perceived as not as adaptable or active. The positive benefits of this trend are seen in the salary profile. Salaries of employees who stay in a company for a couple of years are half that of their counterparts who are more mobile. By switching jobs, a person can undergo deliberate practice on various skills and evolve into a highly skilled performer.

Author's Style

Ericsson is partial to using facts to prove his point which is expected of one who has an academic orientation. Largely, his book is replete with empirical evidences. For instance, he extensively describes research that he personally conducted—a case which he credits to deliberate practice. In particular, the experiment involved training a student to enhance his memorization skills which resulted in his ability to memorize an 82-digit number when prior to this the student could only manage to recall 8 digits. Ericsson likewise cites works of other experts on memory enhancement and the plasticity of the brain. He notes the changes in the mature brain when going through deliberate training. In a research on taxi drivers in London, an increase in the growth of their hippocampus was linked to their driving skills. When Ericsson has no factual evidence—for instance, the facts to disprove that Mozart was naturally gifted, Ericsson provides clues and leaves so the readers arrive at their conclusions.

Author's Perspective

In 1993, the American Psychological Association commissioned Ericsson to conduct research on his innovative concept of deliberate practice. His pioneering study was popularized not only by psychologists but by media practitioners as well. Canadian journalist, Malcolm Gladwell's bestselling book Outliers adopts and to some extent expands on Ericsson's theory that practice indeed makes perfect. But in Peak, Ericsson qualifies some aspects of the concept of deliberate practice that are misinterpreted in Outliers. He adamantly argues against the magical power of a 10,000- hour skills practice and stands pat on his belief that it does not warrant expert performance. When done over time—Ericsson is quick to add that there is no telling how long training should take—it is deliberate and purposeful practice which makes one a top performer.

Connect with Ant Hive Media!

Thank you for reading!

We hope you enjoyed this summary version of the book and took something away from it.
Let us know what you learned and help others by leaving a review.

Want more?

Visit
www.anthivemedia.com/freesummaries
to receive your pack of (5) e-book summaries
FREE!

Check us out on Instagram:
www.instagram.com/anthivemedia/

Follow along on Facebook:
www.facebook.com/AntHiveMediaSocial

Customers Who Bought This Summary Also Bought

Cal Newport's Deep Work: Rules for Focused Success in a Distracted World Summary

Malcolm Gladwell's Blink: The Power of Thinking Without Thinking

Eric Schmidt and Jonathan Rosenberg's HOW GOOGLE WORKS Summary

Eric Ries' The Lean Startup: How Today's Entrepreneurs Use Continuous Innovation to Create Radically Successful Business Summary

Ed Catmull & Amy Wallace's Creativity, Inc: Overcoming the Unseen Forces that Stand in the Way of True Inspiration Summary

Adam Grant's Originals: How Non-Conformists Move the World Summary

Martin Ford's Rise of the Robots Summary: Technology and the Threat of a Jobless Future

Made in the USA
Middletown, DE
22 November 2016